THE TRUTH
OF BEING

Reference Notes

"Love Thy Neighbor" was originally
published in 1958 as chapter 5 in
Practicing the Presence, by Joel Goldsmith.

"The Relationship of Oneness" was originally
published in 1959 as chapter 11 in
The Art of Spiritual Healing, by Joel Goldsmith.

Other Titles in This Series

THE TRUTH
OF BEING

Joel S. Goldsmith

Acropolis Books, Publisher
Longboat Key, Florida

The Truth of Being by Joel S. Goldsmith

Love Thy Neighbor, from Chapter 5 of Practicing the
Presence by Joel S. Goldsmith, © 1986 Emma A. Goldsmith.

The Relationship of Oneness, from Chapter 11 of The Art
of Spiritual Healing by Joel S. Goldsmith, © 1987 Emma A.
Goldsmith

Acropolis Books, Inc.
Longboat Key, Florida
www.acropolisbooks.com

Except the Lord build the house,
they labour in vain that build it.

Psalm 127

Illumination dissolves all material ties and binds men together with the golden chains of spiritual understanding; it acknowledges only the leadership of the Christ; it has no ritual or rule but the divine, impersonal universal Love; no other worship than the inner Flame that is ever lit at the shrine of Spirit. This union is the free state of spiritual brotherhood. The only restraint is the discipline of Soul; therefore, we know liberty without license; we are a united universe without physical limits; a divine service to God without ceremony or creed. The illumined walk without fear – by Grace.

From the *The Infinite Way* by Joel S. Goldsmith

LOVE THY NEIGHBOR

Thou shalt love the Lord thy God with all thy heart, and with all thy soul, and with all thy mind.

This is the first and great commandment.

And the second is like unto it, Thou shalt love thy neighbor as thyself.

Matthew 22:37-39

THE TWO GREAT commandments of the Master form the basis of our work. In the first and great commandment, we are taught that there is no power apart from God. Our realization must always be that the Father within us, the Infinite Invisible, is our life, our Soul, our supply, our fortress, and our high tower. Next in importance is the commandment to "love thy neighbor as thyself," and its corollary that we should do unto others as we would have others do unto us.

What is love in the spiritual sense? What is the love which is God? As we remember how God was with Abraham, with Moses in the wilderness, with Jesus, John, and Paul, ministering to them, the word "love" takes on a new meaning. We see that this love is not something far-off, nor is it anything that can come to us. It is already a part of our being, already established within us; and more than that, it is universal and impersonal. As this universal and impersonal love flows out from us, we begin to love our neighbor, because it is impossible to feel this love for God within us and not love our fellow man.

> *If a man say, I love God, and hateth his brother, he is a liar: for he that loveth not his brother whom he hath seen, how can he love God whom he hath not seen?*
>
> I John 4:20

God and man are one, and there is no way to love God without some of that love flowing out to our neighbor.

Let us understand that anything of which we can become aware is a neighbor, whether it appears as a person, place, or thing. Every idea in consciousness is a neighbor. We can love that neighbor as we see him or it possessing no power except that which comes from God. When we see God as the cause and our neighbor, as that which is in and of God, then we are loving our neighbor, whether that neighbor appears as a friend, relative, enemy, animal, flower, or stone. In such loving, which understands all neighbors to be of God, derived of God-substance, we find that every idea in consciousness takes its rightful place. Those neighbors who are a part of our experience find their way to us, and those who are not are removed. Let us resolve loving our neighbor into a spiritual activity, beholding love as the substance of all that is, no matter what the form may be. As we rise above our humanhood to a higher dimension of life in which we understand our neighbor to be pure spiritual being, God-governed, neither good nor bad, we are truly loving.

Love is the law of God. When we are in tune with divine love, loving whether it be friend or enemy, then love is a gentle thing bringing peace. But it is gentle only while we are in tune with it. It is like electricity. Electricity is very gentle and kind, giving light, warmth, and energy, as long as the laws of electricity are obeyed. The minute they are violated or played with, electricity becomes a double-edged sword. The law of love is as inexorable as the law of electricity.

Now let us be very clear on one point: We cannot harm anybody, and nobody can harm us. No one can injure us, but we injure ourselves by a violation of the law of love. The penalty is always upon the one who is doing the evil, never upon the one to whom it is done. The injustice we do to another reacts upon ourselves; the theft from another robs ourselves. The law of love makes it inevitable that the person who seems to have been harmed is really blessed. He has a greater opportunity to rise than ever before, and usually some greater benefit comes to him than he had ever dreamed possible; whereas the perpetrator of the evil deed is haunted by memories until that day comes when he can forgive himself. The whole proof that this is true is in the one word "Self." God is our Selfhood. God is my Selfhood and God is your Selfhood. God constitutes my being, for God is my life, my Soul, my spirit, my mind, and my activity. God is my Self. That Self is the only Self there is—my Self and your Self. If I rob your Self, whom am I robbing? My Self. If I lie about your Self, about whom am I lying? My Self. If I cheat your Self, whom do I cheat? My Self. There is only one Self, and that which I do to another, I do to my Self.

The Master taught this lesson in the twenty-fifth chapter of Matthew, when he said: "Inasmuch as ye have done it unto one of the least of these my brethren, ye have done it unto me." What I do of good for you, I am not doing for you at all; it is for my benefit. What I do of evil to you, will not hurt you, for you will find a way to recover from it; the reaction will be on me. We must come to the place where we actually believe and can say with our whole heart: "There is only one Self. The injustice that I am doing to another I am doing to myself. The lack of thoughtfulness that I show to another, I am showing to myself." In such recognition, the true meaning of doing unto others as we would have them do unto us is revealed.

God is individual being, which means that God is the only Self, and there is no way for any hurt or evil to enter to defile the infinite purity of the Soul of God, nor anything at which evil can strike or to which it can attach itself. When the Master repeated the age-old wisdom: "Therefore all things whatsoever ye would that men should do to you, do ye even so to them: for this is the law and the prophets," he was giving us a principle. Unless we do unto others as we would have others do unto us, we injure, not the others, but ourselves. In this present state of human consciousness, it is true that the evil thoughts, dishonest acts, and thoughtless words we inflict upon others do harm them temporarily, but always in the end it will be found that the injury was not nearly so great to them as it was to ourselves.

In the days to come, when men recognize the great truth that God is the Selfhood of every individual, the evil aimed at us from another will never touch us, but will immediately rebound upon the one who sends it. In the degree that we recognize God as our individual being, we realize that no weapon that is formed against us can prosper because the only *I* is God. There will be no fear of what man can do to us, since our Selfhood is God and cannot be harmed. As soon as the first realization of this truth comes to us, we no longer concern ourselves with what our neighbor does to us. Morning, noon, and night we must watch our thoughts, our words, and our deeds to make certain that we, ourselves, are not responsible for anything of a negative nature which would have undesirable repercussions.

This will not result in our being good because we fear evil consequences. The revelation of the one Self goes far deeper than that: It enables us to see that God is our Selfhood, and that anything of an erroneous or negative nature which emanates from any individual has power only in the degree that we ourselves give it power. So it is that whatever of good or of evil we do unto others, we do unto the Christ of our own being. "Inasmuch as ye have done it unto one of the least of these my brethren, ye have done it unto me." In that realization, we shall see that this is the truth about all men, and that the only road to a successful and satisfying life is to understand our neighbor to be our Self.

The Master has instructed us specifically as to the ways in which we can serve our fellow man. He emphasized the idea of service. His whole mission was the healing of the sick, the raising of the dead, and the feeding of the poor. The moment that we make ourselves avenues for the out-flow of divine love, from that very moment, we begin serving each other, expressing love, devotion, and sharing, all in the name of the Father.

Let us follow the example of the Master and seek no glory for ourselves. With him, always, it was the Father who doeth the works. There is never any room for self-justification, or self-righteousness, or self-glorification in the performance of any kind of service. Sharing with one another should not be reduced to mere philanthropy. Some people wonder why they find themselves left with nothing when they have always been so charitable. They come upon lean days because they believe that they have given of their own possessions; whereas the truth is that "the earth is the Lord's and the fullness thereof." If we express our love for our fellow man, realizing that we are giving nothing of ourselves, but all is of the Father, from whom every good and perfect gift comes, we shall then be able to give freely and discover that with all our giving there yet remain twelve baskets full left over. To believe that we are giving of our property, our time, or our strength reduces such giving to philanthropy and brings with it no reward. The true giving comes when giving is a recognition that "the earth is the Lord's," and that whether we give of our time or our effort, we are not giving of our own, but of the Lord's. Then are we expressing the love which is of God.

As we forgive, divine love is flowing out from us. As we pray for our enemies, we are loving divinely. Praying for our friends profiteth nothing. The greatest rewards of prayer come when we learn to set aside specific periods every day to pray for those who despitefully use us, to pray for those who persecute us, to pray for those who are our enemies— not only personal enemies because there are some people who have no personal enemies, but religious, racial, or national enemies. We learn to pray, "Father, forgive them; for they know not what they do." When we pray for our enemies, when we pray that their eyes be opened to the Truth, many times these enemies become our friends.

We begin this practice with our personal relationships. If there are individuals with whom we are not on harmonious terms, we find, as we turn within and pray that brotherly love and harmony be established between us, that instead of enemies, we come into a relationship of spiritual brotherhood with them. Our relationship with everybody then takes on a harmony and a heretofore unknown joy.

This is not possible as long as we feel antagonism toward anyone. If we are harboring within us personal animosity, or if we are indulging in national or religious hatred, prejudice, or bigotry, our prayers are worthless. We must go to God with clean hands in order to pray, and to approach God with clean hands, we must relinquish our animosities. Within ourselves, we must first of all pray the prayer of forgiveness for those who have offended us, since they know not what they do; and secondly, acknowledge within ourselves: "I stand in relationship to God as a son, and therefore, I stand in relationship to every man as a brother." When we have established that state of purity within ourselves, then we can ask the Father:

Give me grace; give me understanding; give me peace; give me this day my daily bread— give me this day spiritual bread, spiritual understanding. Give me forgiveness, even for those harmless trespasses which I have unwittingly committed.

The person who turns within for light, for grace, for understanding, and for forgiveness never fails in his prayers.

The law of God is the law of love, the law of loving our enemies—not fearing them, not hating them, but loving them. No matter what an individual does to us, we are not to strike back. To resist evil, to retaliate, or to seek revenge is to acknowledge evil as reality. If we resist evil, if we refute it, if we avenge ourselves, or if we strike back, we are not praying for them which despitefully use us and persecute us.

How can we say that we acknowledge good alone, God, as the only power, if we hate our neighbor or do evil to anyone? Christ is the true identity and to recognize an identity other than Christ is to withdraw ourselves from Christ-consciousness.

Love your enemies, bless them that curse you, do good to them that hate you, and pray for them which despitefully use you, and persecute you;

That ye may be the children of your Father which is in heaven: for he maketh his sun to rise on the evil and on the good, and sendeth rain on the just and on the unjust.

Matthew 5:44-45

There is no other way to be the Christ, the Son of God. The Christ-mind has in it no criticism, no judgment, no condemnation, but beholds the Christ of God as the activity of individual being, as your Soul and mine. Human eyes do not comprehend this because as human beings, we are good and bad; but spiritually, we are the Sons of God, and through spiritual consciousness we can discern the spiritual good in each other. There is no room in spiritual living for persecution, hatred, judgment, or condemnation of any person or group of people. It is not only inconsistent, but hypocritical to talk about the Christ and our great love for God in one breath, and, in the next breath, speak disparagingly of a neighbor who is of a different race, creed, nationality, political affiliation, or economic status. One cannot be the child of God as long as he persecutes or hates anyone or anything, but only as he lives in a consciousness of no judgment or condemnation.

The usual interpretation of "judge not" is that we are not to judge evil of anyone. We must go much further than that; we dare not judge good of anyone either. We must be as careful not to call anyone good as we are not to call anyone evil. We should not label anyone or anything as evil, but likewise, we should not label anyone or anything as good. The Master said: "Why callest thou me good? there is none good but one, that is God." It is the height of egotism to say: "I am good; I have understanding; I am moral; I am generous; I am benevolent." If any qualities of good are manifesting through us, let us not call ourselves good, but recognize these qualities as the activity of God. "Son, thou art ever with me, and all that I have is thine." All the good of the Father is expressed through me.

One of the basic principles of The Infinite Way is that good humanhood is not sufficient to ensure our entry into the spiritual kingdom, nor to bring us into oneness with cosmic law. It is undoubtedly better to be a good human being than a bad one, just as it is better to be a healthy human being than a sick one; but achieving health or achieving goodness, in and of itself, is not spiritual living. Spiritual living comes only when we have risen above human good and human evil and realize: "There are not good human beings or bad human beings. Christ is the only identity." Then we look out on the world and see neither good men and women nor bad men and women, but recognize Christ alone as the reality of being.

Therefore if thou bring thy gift to the altar, and there rememberest that thy brother hath ought against thee;

Leave there thy gift before the altar, and go thy way; first be reconciled to thy brother, and then come and offer thy gift.

Matthew 5:23-24

If we are holding anyone in condemnation as a human being, good or bad, just or unjust, we have not made peace with our brother and we are not ready for the prayer of communion with the Infinite. We rise above the righteousness of the scribes and Pharisees only when we stop seeing good and evil, and stop boasting about goodness as if any of us could be good. Goodness is a quality and activity of God alone, and because it is, it is universal.

Let us never accept a human being into our consciousness who needs healing, employing, or enriching because if we do, we are his enemy instead of his friend. If there is any man, woman, or child we believe to be sick, sinning, or dying, let us do no praying until we have made peace with that brother. The peace we must make with that brother is to ask forgiveness for making the mistake of sitting in judgment on any individual because everyone is God in expression. All is God manifested. God alone constitutes this universe; God constitutes the life, the mind, and the Soul of every individual.

"Thou shalt not bear false witness against thy neighbor" has a much broader connotation than merely not spreading rumors or indulging in gossip about our neighbor. We are not to hold our neighbor in humanhood. If we say, "I have a good neighbor," we are bearing false witness against him just as much as if we said, "I have a bad neighbor," because we are acknowledging a state of humanhood, sometimes good and sometimes bad, but never spiritual. To bear false witness against our neighbor is to declare that he is human, that he is finite, that he has failings, that he is something less than the very Son of God. Every time we acknowledge humanhood, we violate cosmic law. Every time we acknowledge our neighbor as sinful, poor, sick, or dead, every time we acknowledge him to be other than the Son of God, we are bearing false witness against our neighbor.

In the violation of that cosmic law, we bring about our own punishment. God does not punish us. We punish ourselves because if I say that you are poor, I virtually am saying that I am poor. There is only one I and one Selfhood; whatever truth I know about *you* is the truth about *me*. If I accept the belief of poverty in the world, that reacts upon me. If I say that you are sick or that you are not kind, I am accepting a quality apart from God, an activity apart from God, and in that way I am condemning myself because there is but one Self. Ultimately, I convict myself by bearing false witness against my neighbor and I am the one who suffers the consequences.

The only way to avoid bearing false witness against our neighbor is to realize that the Christ is our neighbor, that our neighbor is a spiritual being, the Son of God, just as we are. He may not know it; we may not know it; but the truth is: *I* am Spirit; *I* am Soul; *I* am consciousness; *I* am God expressed—and so is he, whether he is good or bad, friend or enemy, next door or across the seas.

In the Sermon on the Mount, the Master gave us a guide and a code of human conduct to follow while developing spiritual consciousness. The Infinite Way emphasizes spiritual values, a spiritual code, which automatically results in good humanhood.

Good humanhood is a natural consequence of spiritual identification. It would be difficult to understand that the Christ is the Soul and the life of individual being, and then quarrel with our neighbor or slander him. We place our faith, trust, and confidence in the Infinite Invisible, and we do not take into consideration human circumstances and conditions. Then, when we do come to human circumstances or conditions, we see them in their true relationship. When we say, "Thou shalt love thy neighbor as thyself," we are not speaking of human love, affection, or friendliness; we are holding our neighbor in spiritual identity, and then we see the effect of this right identification in the human picture.

Many times we find it difficult to love our neighbor because we believe that our neighbor is standing between us and our good. Let me assure you that this is far from true. No outer influence for good or evil can act upon us. We ourselves release our good. To understand the full meaning of this requires a transition in consciousness. As human beings, we think that there are those individuals in the world who can, if they would, be good to us; or we think that there are some who are an influence for evil, harm, or destruction. How can this possibly be true if God is the only influence in our life—God, who is "closer. . . than breathing, and nearer than hands or feet"? The only influence is that of the Father within, which is always good. "Thou couldest have no power at all against me, except it were given thee from above."

When we realize that our life is unfolding from within our own being, we come to the realization that no one on earth has ever hurt us, and no one on earth has ever helped us. Every hurt that has ever come into our experience has been the direct result of our inability to behold this universe as spiritual. We have looked upon it with either praise or condemnation, and no matter which it was, we have brought a penalty upon ourselves. If we look back over the years, we could almost blueprint the reasons for every bit of discord that has come into our experience. In every case, it is the same thing—always because we saw somebody or something that was not spiritual.

Nobody can benefit us; nobody can harm us. It is what goes out from us that returns to bless or to condemn us. We create good and we create evil. We create our own good and we create our own evil. God does not do either: God *is*. God is a principle of love. If we are at-one with that principle, then we bring good into our experience; but if we are not at-one with that principle, we bring evil into our experience. Whatever is flowing out from our consciousness, that which is going forth in secret, is being shown to the world in outward manifestation.

Whatever emanates from God in the consciousness of man, individually or collectively, is power. What is it that emanates from God and operates in the consciousness of man but love, truth, completeness, perfection, wholeness—all of the Christ-qualities? Because there is only one God, one infinite Power, love must be the controlling emotion in the hearts and souls of every person on the face of the globe.

Now in contrast to that, are those other thoughts of fear, doubt, hate, jealousy, envy, and animality, which are probably uppermost in the consciousness of many of the people of the world. We, as truth-seekers, belong to a very small minority of those who have received the impartation that the evil thoughts of men are not power; they have no control over us. Not all the evil or false thinking on earth has any power over you or over me when we understand that love is the only power. There is no power in hate; there is no power in animosity; there is no power in resentment, lust, greed, or jealousy.

There are few people in the world who are able to accept the teaching that love is the only power and who are willing to "become as a little child." Those who do accept this basic teaching of the Master, however, are those of whom he said:

> ... I thank thee, O Father, Lord of heaven and earth, that thou hast hid these things from the wise and prudent, and hast revealed them unto babes: even so, Father; for so it seemed good in thy sight.
>
> ... blessed are the eyes which see the things that ye see: For I tell you, that many prophets and

kings have desired to see those things which ye see,
and have not seen them; and to hear those things
which ye hear, and have not heard them.

Luke 10:21, 23, 24

Once we accept this all-important teaching of the Master and our eyes see beyond the appearance, we shall consciously realize daily that every person in the world is empowered with love from on High, and that the love in his consciousness is the only power, a power of good unto you, unto me, and unto himself; but that the evil in human thought, whether it takes the form of greed, jealousy, lust, or mad ambition, is not power, is not to be feared or hated.

Our method of loving our brother as ourselves is in this realization: The good in our brother is of God and is power; the evil in our brother is not power, not power against us, and in the last analysis, not even power against him, once he awakens to the truth. To love our brother means to know the truth about our brother: to know that that in him, which is of God, is power and that in him, which is not of God, is not power. Then are we truly loving our brother. Centuries of orthodox teaching have instilled in all the peoples of the world a sense of separation so that they have developed interests separate and apart from one another and also apart from the world at large. When we master the principle of oneness, however, and this principle becomes a conviction deep within us, in that oneness the lion and the lamb can lie down together.

This is proved to be true through an understanding of the correct meaning of the word "*I*." Once we catch the first perception of the truth that the *I* of me is the *I* of you, the Self of me is the Self of you, then we shall see why we have no interests apart from each other. There would be no wars, no conflicts of any kind, if only it could be made clear that the real being of everybody in the universe is the one God, the one Christ, the one Soul, and the one Spirit. What benefits one benefits another because of this oneness.

In that spiritual oneness, we find our peace with one another. If we experiment with this we shall quickly see how true it is. When we go to the market, we realize that everyone we meet is this same one that we are, that the same life animates him, the same Soul, the same love, the same joy, the same peace, the same desire for good. In other words, the same God sits enthroned within all those with whom we come in contact. They may not, at the moment, be conscious of this divine Presence within their being, but they will respond as we recognize It in them. In the business world, whether it is among our co-workers, our employers, or our employees, whether it is among competitors, or whether in management and labor relationships, we maintain this attitude of recognition:

I am you. My interest is your interest; your interest is mine, since the one life animates our being, the one Soul, the one Spirit of God. Anything we do for each other, we do because of the principle that binds us together.

A difference is immediately noticeable in our business relationships, in our relationships with tradespeople, and in our community relationships—ultimately, in national and international relationships. The moment that we give up our human sense of separateness, this principle becomes operative in our experience. It has never failed and it never will fail to bring forth rich fruitage.

Everyone is here on earth but for one purpose, and that purpose is to show forth the glory of God, the divinity and the fullness of God. In that realization, we shall be brought into contact only with those who are a blessing to us as we are a blessing to them.

The moment we look to a person for our good, we may find good today and evil tomorrow. Spiritual good may come *through* you to me from the Father, but it does not come *from* you. You cannot be the source of any good to me, but the Father may use you as an instrument for Its good to flow through you to me. So, as we look at our friends or our family in this light, they become instruments of God, of God's good, reaching us through them. We come under grace by taking the position that all good emanates from the Father within. It may appear to come through countless different people, but it is an emanation of good, of God from within us.

What is the principle? "Love thy neighbor as thyself." In obeying this commandment we love friend and foe; we pray for our enemies; we forgive, though it be seventy times seven; we bear not false witness against our neighbor by holding him in condemnation; we judge not as to good or evil, but see through every appearance to the Christ-identity—the one Self which is your Self and my Self. Then can it be said of us:

> ... *Come, ye blessed of my Father, inherit the kingdom prepared for you from the foundation of the world:*
>
> *For I was an hungered, and ye gave me meat: I was thirsty, and ye gave me drink: I was a stranger, and ye took me in:*
>
> *Naked, and ye clothed me: I was sick, and ye visited me: I was in prison, and ye came unto me.*
>
> *Then shall the righteous answer him, saying, Lord, when saw we thee an hungered, and fed thee? or thirsty, and gave thee drink?*
>
> *When saw we thee a stranger, and took thee in? or naked, and clothed thee?*

Or when saw we thee sick, or in prison, and came unto thee?

And the King shall answer and say unto them, Verily I say unto you, Inasmuch as ye have done it unto one of the least of these my brethren, ye have done it unto me.

Matthew 25:34-40

THE RELATIONSHIP
OF ONENESS

YOUR WORLD AND MINE is an outpicturing of our consciousness: When that consciousness is imbued with truth, our universe expresses harmony, orderliness, prosperity, joy, peace, power, and dominion; when there is an absence of truth in our consciousness—an acceptance of world values and world beliefs—then our world takes on the complexion of the chance, change, and luck characteristic of world belief. All conditions reflect the activity of the consciousness of the individuals concerned.

Your world is embodied in your consciousness; it reflects the state of your consciousness because your consciousness governs your world. Your awareness of truth is the law unto your world; but, on the other hand, your ignorance of truth likewise becomes a law unto it. For example, there is no law of darkness because you know that darkness can be dispelled by the presence of light. Yet in the absence of light, darkness would claim presence; and just so in the absence of truth in your consciousness, ignorance, lies, appearances, discords, and inharmony claim to be present. Therefore, in the absence of the activity of truth in your consciousness, your world will reflect chance, luck, human belief, medical belief, or astrological belief; but the activity of truth operating in and as your consciousness becomes a law of harmony unto everything in your world and makes everything concerning you reflect the harmony of your consciousness.

Suppose that you find yourself in a situation where you are faced with a roomful of people with whom you must work in some capacity or other—talk to them, instruct them, or serve them. As you look at them, they present a variety of appearances—good people, bad, sick, well, rich, and poor. How can you establish a sense of oneness with all these people? To feel a sense of union with any other person means, first of all, that you must make your contact with the Spirit within and find your own completeness; you must make your contact with the Father within, whereupon you automatically become one with every other individual within range of your consciousness.

This is your opportunity to apply the principles of The Infinite Way. Look over or through every person in the room to God:

*God is the animating principle of every
individual; God is the mind of every person here,
the intelligence expressing as person. God is the
only love, and God being infinite, God is all love;
therefore, God is the love of individual being,
and being filled with the love which is God, no
individual can be used as an instrument for hate,
envy, jealousy, or malice.*

Realization such as that will lift you above
personalities into the realm of pure being.

You may be confronted with evidences of
misunderstanding, but what difference does
it make what the appearance is? Right where
that appearance is foisting itself upon your
mind, God is. You are dealing only with God,
not with beliefs, persons, or conditions.

Over and over again it has been proved that
when confronting people who have fallen
prey to anger or when meeting with vicious
animals poised and ready to attack, by merely

holding to the realization of God as the real entity or identity—the real being—God as the only law, the only substance, the only cause, the only effect, what we call healing takes place. This method of treatment never leaves the realm of God, never comes down to the level of man or person or condition or circumstance, nor does it take unemployment, sin, or disease into consideration.

It is so easy to say that this is good and that is evil, this is of God and that is of the devil; but it is when a person or circumstance claims to have the power to crucify or set you free, to cause you trouble, to do this or that to you, that you must take your stand and realize:

My being is in Christ, and as long as I maintain my being in Christ, only the Christ can operate in my consciousness—which is the one consciousness, the consciousness of every person in the world.

In other words, when you look out at this world and see persons or circumstances claiming to have power over you for good or evil, you again must acknowledge that your being is in Christ and only the Christ-inspired can have any influence in your affairs.

Several years ago in a period of distress it came to me that I must love those who hate me, I must give love for ingratitude; and my answer was, "Father, I just can't do it. I don't know how to do it. Yes, I can be a hypocrite and say that I love these people who are hating, condemning, judging, and fighting me; but I can tell you truthfully that I don't—I don't know how to love them. It is true I have no antagonism toward them because I know what motivates them and I do not blame them. If I did not have a little understanding of Your infinite love, I might do the same thing in their position; so I have no sense of judgment or criticism or condemnation of them. I can even say, 'Father, forgive them; for they know not what they do'—but to love them! No, I cannot honestly say that I love them. I just cannot do that. If there is to be any loving, I am perfectly willing to be the avenue through which You, God, can love them through me. If that can be arranged, let's have it that way; but don't ask me to love them because that is beyond my capacity."

It was less than a minute after that that I settled down into a beautiful peace, went to sleep, and awakened completely healed. It is impossible to love ingratitude, injustice, misrepresentation, and lies, but we can be willing to let God take over: "God, You who could love the thief on the cross and the woman taken in adultery, You love these people too."

What was required for the demonstration that I had to make? Was it not the ability to "nothingize" myself, even to the extent of not trying to be self-righteous about loving my enemy? When you say that you are loving your enemy, that is self-righteousness. We have to learn to let God do the loving and be willing to be an instrument through which God's love flows to our friends and to our enemies.

In the world there are good people and bad people, just and unjust people, but when you climb up into that circle of God you find that God is the principle of all people; God is the only principle of people, the animating love and life and truth of all people—those in your business, in your social relationships, and in your home.

Your home is a composite of your consciousness of home. You are the doorkeeper of your household and you should stand guard at the door to see that nothing gets past that door which does not have the right to be there. This door, however, is not a material door. The only door there is, is the door of consciousness, and the only door for which you are responsible is that door. What do you allow to get past your door; your consciousness? Do you accept contagion and infection as power in your home? Are you a party to discord and bickering? You should make it a matter of daily realization that nothing can enter the doorway of consciousness except the truth of being, and that no suggestion of human power, whether physical, material, or mental, is law. Any belief that enters your home must first enter through your consciousness, and the truth of being in your consciousness will act as a law of annihilation to any false belief that would intrude.

Everything that comes within range of your consciousness will take on the nature and character of that consciousness. Your own life is not only affected by what gets past the door of your consciousness, but the life of everyone who has brought himself to your consciousness is affected, and that includes the members of your family and sometimes the members of your community and church. All these look to you for bread; they look to you for the truth of being, but oftentimes your mind is so occupied with concern over your own discords and inharmonies that they are turned away without the divine substance which they sought from you.

Deep within every person is a hunger for the bread of life. Friends, relatives, and even acquaintances who find their way to your home ostensibly seeking companionship, supply, or any form of material good, even though from their point of view that may be their purpose, are in reality longing and craving for the true substance of life, the meat that perisheth not. If you give them money and give them that alone, if you give them your physical, human companionship, and give them that alone, you are giving them a stone: You are not giving them the bread of life; you are not lifting their state of consciousness. This you can do only in the degree that you are specifically entertaining the consciousness of truth within your being as they come to you:

God is the substance and the activity of my home; God is the consciousness of every individual who enters my home, whether it is family or friends. Nothing enters my home to contaminate or violate its sanctity, because God is my only home. As long as my home appears on earth as a material structure, it will express the harmony of God. Those in that home will either reflect that harmony or they will be removed because nothing unlike God can remain in my home—my temple, my being, my body. Anything of a discordant nature that would enter, or might temporarily be permitted to enter, will be removed in its time and in such a way that it will injure no one, but be a blessing to everyone involved.

Since God is my consciousness, nothing can enter that consciousness that "defileth or maketh a lie," and even if I, in my ignorance or human softness, permit something to enter which has no place there, it will not long remain. The consciousness of Truth and Life which I am will heal it or remove it. I am willing that everybody and everything that enters my consciousness shall be either healed or removed. I dare not cling to anyone and say, "With all your faults, I still need you and want you." I take my stand with God and, if necessary, leave father, mother, brother, sister, husband, or wife in order to dwell in the secret place of the most High.

Clinging to that which you know is not right just because of human emotion very often does much to impede your spiritual demonstration. Each one must rely upon inner guidance to determine when to let go of human ties and when not to let go.

Nearly every marriage ceremony contains some version of the statement, "that which God has joined together let no man put asunder." The truth is that what God has joined together, what God has brought together in oneness and unity, no man can put asunder. It would be an utter impossibility for man to have power over God and over God's work. No man has the power to undo the work of God. In the world of appearances, there can be temporary strife, discord and inharmony—and there will be, but not for you if you climb into that circle of God and there live in the constant realization that what

God has made is forever, and what God has brought together no man can put asunder.

In dealing with a marital problem, you would realize that since God is one, the only relationship that exists is a relationship of oneness, and there can be no division or separation in that oneness—no inharmony or discord in one. The moment there are two, there can be any kind of discord and inharmony, but that is impossible in oneness.

Many people believe that a realization such as this would ensure a couple's remaining together, and that, therefore, no divorce or separation could possibly follow. Nothing could be further from the truth. A couple may be married and may be legally one, and yet they may not actually be one in their being— they may not be spiritually one. Therefore, this realization of oneness might bring about a separation or divorce much more quickly than would otherwise be the case, freeing both husband and wife from the yoke of inharmony and discord and enabling both to find their oneness elsewhere. No two people can realize oneness or true happiness when life resolves itself into a continuous battle of misunderstandings and disagreements. The marital relationship without love is a sin.

A practitioner of spiritual healing should never intrude into the family life of any person or of any couple, nor judge humanly as to whether two people should get married, remain married, be separated, or divorced. That is not the business of a spiritual healer, and, furthermore, there is no easy way of knowing from outward appearances what the truth of the situation is. In all cases of marital discord and inharmony, hold to the fact that God is the only one and there is only one marriage, the mystical marriage. Such a marriage is God-ordained, and no man can rend it asunder.

Sometimes the very best way that God can maintain that oneness is by severing the human or legal tie. Never believe for a minute that just knowing oneness will keep all marriages together, because it will not. Knowing oneness will keep a person one with his good; and if that good means celibacy, marriage, separation, or divorce, that is what will happen. No one has the right to outline how a demonstration is to take place because everything must unfold in accordance with spiritual good, not in accordance with some human being's idea of what constitutes good. No one should set himself up as being competent to decide what is humanly good.

It is unwise to attempt to protect loved ones from discords and inharmonies which, knowingly or unknowingly, they have brought and are bringing upon themselves. It is better to give up anxious concern, loose them, and let them live with some of their discords, because the overprotection which would keep them from the results of their own conduct is often the stumbling block which prevents them from awakening to the truth of being. Their very suffering may be the needling necessary to awaken them. Each one of us has to learn the lesson of "loose him, and let him go." Loose your loved ones into Christ; loose them into God; and let the law of God govern.

Regardless of the amount of spiritual realization attained by some people and the measure of its practice in daily life, there are always those who for one reason or another cannot or will not respond. The greatest known witness to the spiritual life was the Master, Christ Jesus, and yet even he had his Judas, his doubting Thomas, his denying Peter, and his disciples who fell asleep in the Garden. Undoubtedly both Peter and Thomas awakened and atoned for their temporary lapse. Of Judas, there is no proof of any awakening to this spiritual light. Furthermore, there was a time when the spiritual impetus found no answer in Saul of Tarsus, and yet, at a certain given moment, he not only responded to it but he became a great living witness to it.

Therefore, no one need despair if those in his family, his church group, in his nation, or in the world at large are not responding at this moment to the spiritual impulse. In their own time they will. With some of them it may take days, weeks, months, years; and with some it may take many lifetimes to come. But sooner or later every knee will bend—every knee. At some time or other, all men will be taught of God.

People believe that they are held back because of the lack of demonstration of someone around them, or that for one reason or another the lack of demonstration on the part of someone else may have an adverse influence upon them. That could never be true unless they themselves permitted it. Each one is responsible for his own spiritual demonstration, and it is useless to blame the other fellow for a lack of spiritual courage.

No less an authority than the Master has taught that in order to attain the stature of Christhood, it is necessary to leave mother, father, brother, sister "for my sake." Why not face the fact that most people are not yet ready to leave those who they believe are acting in such a way as to hold back their demonstration? So no one should blame anyone—not even himself—but quickly realize that only the acceptance of a universal belief in a selfhood apart from God could hypnotize him into believing that any influence outside his own being could act upon him. How could anyone influence, help, or hinder another person's demonstration? How is it possible for anyone to come between him and his realization of Christhood? That can only be if there is a dependence on a human being.

If men and women accept the universal belief that their support and supply come from husband, wife, investments, or business, they have brought themselves under the law. Before people have any knowledge of spiritual wisdom, such a reliance is natural; but after they have learned the truth of their identity as being one with the Father, if they then persist in placing their "faith in princes"— their reliance on friends or family—instead of freeing themselves and living under grace, they will continue to live under the human law of limitation. In spiritual living there is no dependence upon any person or thing: There is a sharing, but there is never dependence. Whatever is shared with another is shared from the infinite bounty of God:

"I and my Father are one": That is my relationship to God, and that is God's relationship to me. It has nothing to do with any person: It has nothing to do with relatives, friends, or associates. My good is in no way dependent on them, nor is their good dependent on me. My good is God's allness made manifest as my individual being.

When this oneness is glimpsed, every relationship becomes one of friendship, joy, and co-operation. If our dependence is not on others, then no lack or loss would be suffered if our relationships with others were wiped away because good is inherent in our relationship to God, and it does not lie within anyone's power to lose the relationship of joint-heir with Christ in God. The human picture does not testify to that because, in order to benefit by the relationship of Father and son, an activity of truth must take place in individual consciousness.

When you learn to "call no man on earth your father," automatically every man, woman, and child on this earth become your brother and sister. According to human testimony, you may be an only child and you may have no relatives on earth, but once you have agreed to "call no man on earth your father," that is no longer true because you have made a brother and sister of everybody in this universe. People who have looked upon you as a stranger suddenly feel, "I know this person; I feel as if I have always known him." Even though you are not blood-brothers or sisters no barrier exists between you, because now a higher relationship than that of blood-brother or sister has been established: Now you are brothers and sisters by divine ordinance.

There is a bond, a spiritual tie, which binds together all the children of God. This is not a tie to human beings or mortals, and that is why those who persist in remaining on the human or mortal level ultimately drift out of the experience of the more spiritually illumined. Each one draws unto himself those with whom he is spiritually united, his spiritual brothers and sisters; but those who live and insist on living on the mortal or material plane sooner or later drift away from him, and sometimes the greatest heartaches come from trying to hold on to them.

Along the way, you may meet with falsehood, deception, and vilification; sometimes your friends and relatives are asleep, not upholding you, sometimes even resisting or obstructing you. You must reach the point in your unfoldment where that is of no consequence to you. It makes no difference in your life who fails you: It makes a difference only to them because they have failed in their demonstration of their Christhood, but it will make no difference to you if you have learned your relationship to God.

Since God is the life, wisdom, activity, and supply of your being, you have no demonstration to make which is dependent upon anyone here on earth. You are spiritually fed, clothed, and housed. Your utter and complete reliance is on this truth that all that the Father has is yours. If the whole earth were wiped away, this one truth

58

would remain, "I and my Father are one," and all that the Father has would still be yours.

When the Master taught his disciples to leave mother, brother, sister for his sake, he did not mean that they should leave those of their spiritual household. "Who is my mother, or my brethren? And he looked round about on them which sat about him, and said, Behold my mother and my brethren! For whosoever shall do the will of God, the same is my brother, and my sister, and mother." All who can meet together on a spiritual level of love are bound together from now until eternity, sharing forever with each other.

Printed in Great Britain
by Amazon